JAKE BUGG SHANGRI LA

WISE PUBLICATIONS
part of The Music Sales Group
London / New York / Paris / Sydney / Copenhagen / Berlin / Madrid / Hong Kong / Tokyo

Published by
Wise Publications
14-15 Berners Street, London W1T 3LJ, UK.

Exclusive Distributors:
Music Sales Limited
Distribution Centre, Newmarket Road,
Bury St Edmunds, Suffolk IP33 3YB, UK.
Music Sales Pty Limited
Units 3-4, 17 Willfox Street, Condell Park,
NSW 2200, Australia.

Order No. AM1009613
ISBN: 978-1-78305-738-2
This book © Copyright 2014 Wise Publications,
a division of Music Sales Limited.

Edited by Adrian Hopkins.
Music arranged by Matt Cowe.
Music processed by Paul Ewers Music Design.
Photography by Kevin Westenberg.
Printed in the EU.

Your Guarantee of Quality

As publishers, we strive to produce every book
to the highest commercial standards.

This book has been carefully designed to minimise awkward
page turns and to make playing from it a real pleasure.

Particular care has been given to specifying acid-free, neutral-sized
paper made from pulps which have not been elemental chlorine bleached.
This pulp is from farmed sustainable forests and was produced
with special regard for the environment.

Throughout, the printing and binding have been planned to ensure a sturdy,
attractive publication which should give years of enjoyment.
If your copy fails to meet our high standards,
please inform us and we will gladly replace it.

www.musicsales.com

GUITAR TABLATURE EXPLAINED

Guitar music can be explained in three different ways: on a musical stave, in tablature, and in rhythm slashes.

RHYTHM SLASHES: are written above the stave. Strum chords in the rhythm indicated. Round noteheads indicate single notes.

THE MUSICAL STAVE: shows pitches and rhythms and is divided by lines into bars. Pitches are named after the first seven letters of the alphabet.

TABLATURE: graphically represents the guitar fingerboard. Each horizontal line represents a string, and each number represents a fret.

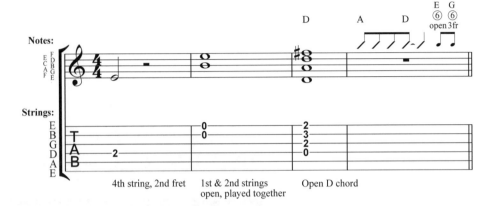

4th string, 2nd fret   1st & 2nd strings open, played together   Open D chord

Definitions for special guitar notation

SEMI-TONE BEND: Strike the note and bend up a semi-tone (½ step).

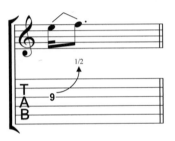

WHOLE-TONE BEND: Strike the note and bend up a whole-tone (full step).

GRACE NOTE BEND: Strike the note and bend as indicated. Play the first note as quickly as possible.

QUARTER-TONE BEND: Strike the note and bend up a ¼ step

BEND & RELEASE: Strike the note and bend up as indicated, then release back to the original note.

COMPOUND BEND & RELEASE: Strike the note and bend up and down in the rhythm indicated.

PRE-BEND: Bend the note as indicated, then strike it.

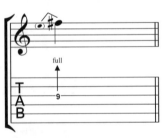

PRE-BEND & RELEASE: Bend the note as indicated. Strike it and release the note back to the original pitch.

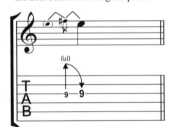

HAMMER-ON: Strike the first note with one finger, then sound the second note (on the same string) with another finger by fretting it without picking.

PULL-OFF: Place both fingers on the note to be sounded, strike the first note and without picking, pull the finger off to sound the second note.

LEGATO SLIDE (GLISS): Strike the first note and then slide the same fret-hand finger up or down to the second note. The second note is not struck.

MUFFLED STRINGS: A percussive sound is produced by laying the first hand across the string(s) without depressing, and striking them with the pick hand.

NATURAL HARMONIC: Strike the note while the fret-hand lightly touches the string directly over the fret indicated.

PICK SCRAPE: The edge of the pick is rubbed down (or up) the string, producing a scratchy sound.

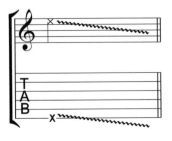

PALM MUTING: The note is partially muted by the pick hand lightly touching the string(s) just before the bridge.

SHIFT SLIDE (GLISS & RESTRIKE) Same as legato slide, except the second note is struck.

TAP HARMONIC: The note is fretted normally and a harmonic is produced by tapping or slapping the fret indicated in brackets (which will be twelve frets higher than the fretted note.)

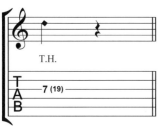

TAPPING: Hammer ('tap') the fret indicated with the pick-hand index or middle finger and pull-off to the note fretted by the fret hand.

PINCH HARMONIC: The note is fretted normally and a harmonic is produced by adding the edge of the thumb or the tip of the index finger of the pick hand to the normal pick attack.

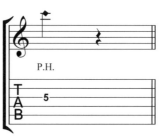

ARTIFICIAL HARMONIC: The note fretted normally and a harmonic is produced by gently resting the pick hand's index finger directly above the indicated fret (in brackets) while plucking the appropriate string.

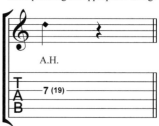

TRILL: Very rapidly alternate between the notes indicated by continuously hammering-on and pulling-off.

RAKE: Drag the pick across the strings with a single motion.

TREMOLO PICKING: The note is picked as rapidly and continously as possible.

ARPEGGIATE: Play the notes of the chord indicated by quickly rolling them from bottom to top.

SWEEP PICKING: Rhythmic downstroke and/or upstroke motion across the strings.

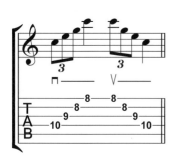

VIBRATO DIVE BAR AND RETURN: The pitch of the note or chord is dropped a specific number of steps (in rhythm) then returned to the original pitch.

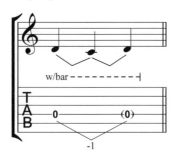

VIBRATO BAR SCOOP: Depress the bar just before striking the note, then quickly release the bar.

VIBRATO BAR DIP: Strike the note and then immediately drop a specific number of steps, then release back to the original pitch.

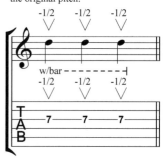

Additional musical definitions

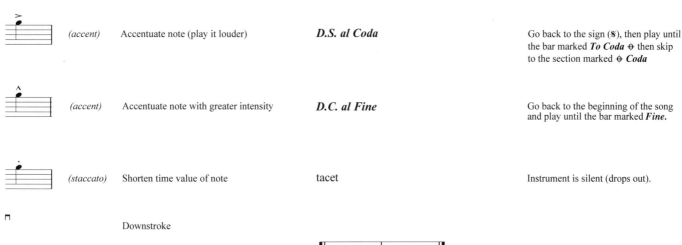

> (accent)	Accentuate note (play it louder)	**D.S. al Coda**
^ (accent)	Accentuate note with greater intensity	**D.C. al Fine**
. (staccato)	Shorten time value of note	tacet
⊓	Downstroke	
V	Upstroke	

D.S. al Coda — Go back to the sign (𝄋), then play until the bar marked **To Coda** ⊕ then skip to the section marked ⊕ **Coda**

D.C. al Fine — Go back to the beginning of the song and play until the bar marked **Fine.**

tacet — Instrument is silent (drops out).

Repeat bars between signs

When a repeat section has different endings, play the first ending only the first time and the second ending only the second time.

NOTE: Tablature numbers in brackets mean:
1. The note is sustained, but a new articulation (such as hammer-on or slide) begins
2. A note may be fretted but not necessarily played.

THERE'S A BEAST AND WE ALL FEED IT

Words & Music by Jake Bugg & Iain Archer

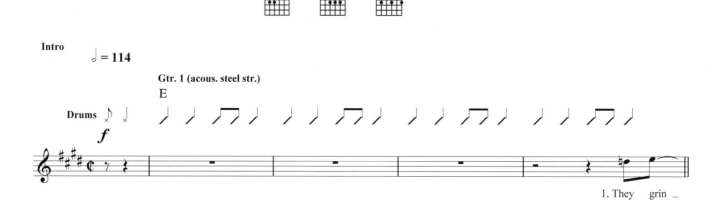

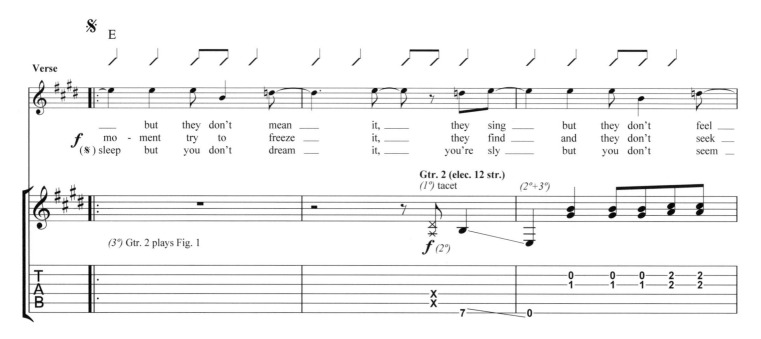

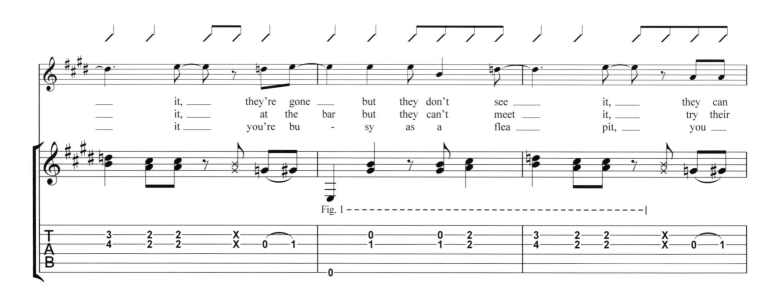

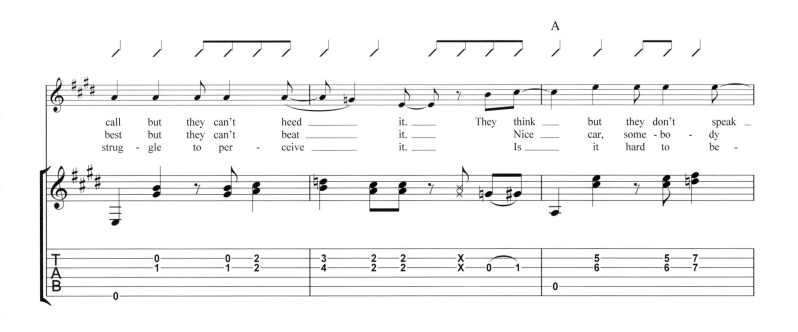

call but they can't heed _____ it. _____ They think ___ but they don't speak ___
best but they can't beat _____ it. _____ Nice ___ car, some-bo-dy
strug - gle to per - ceive _____ it. _____ Is _____ it hard to be -

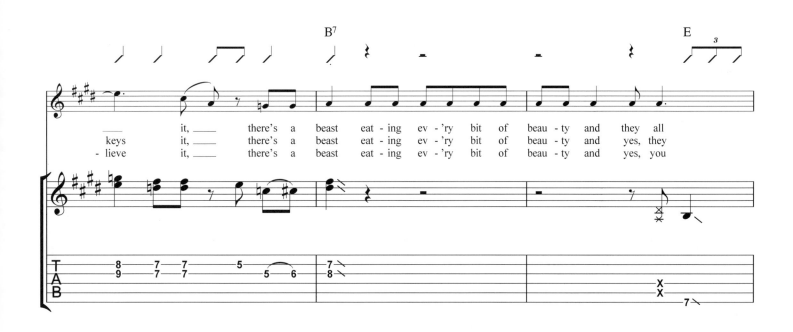

_____ it, _____ there's a beast eat - ing ev - 'ry bit of beau - ty and they all
keys it, _____ there's a beast eat - ing ev - 'ry bit of beau - ty and yes, they
- lieve it, _____ there's a beast eat - ing ev - 'ry bit of beau - ty and yes, you

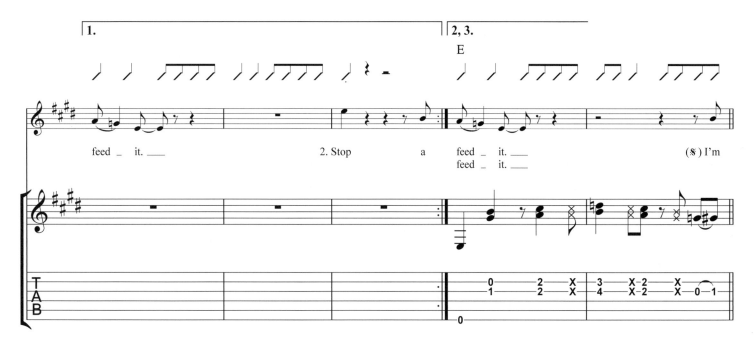

feed _ it. ____   2. Stop   a   feed _ it. ____   (𝄋) I'm
                                                     feed _ it. ____

SLUMVILLE SUNRISE

Words & Music by Jake Bugg & Iain Archer

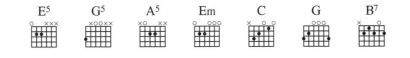

That drum just keeps on bang - ing. They must be buzz - ing out their minds, like bees__

I clench my fists and feet, I'm try - ing to cry__ out loud, make__

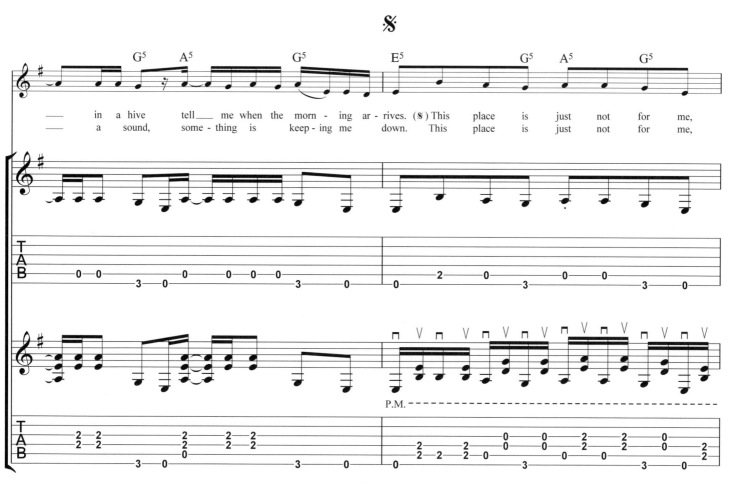

__ in a hive tell__ me when the morn - ing ar - rives. (%) This place is just not for me,

__ a sound, some - thing is keep - ing me down. This place is just not for me,

P.M. -

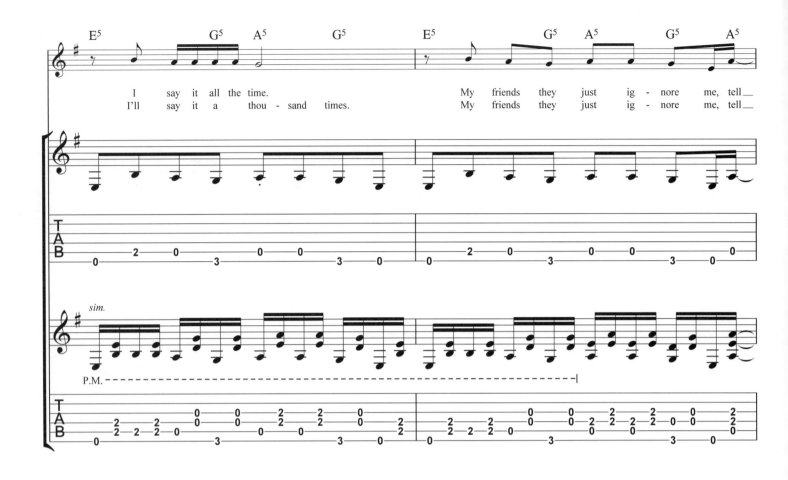

I say it all the time.
I'll say it a thou - sand times.
My friends they just ig - nore me, tell___
My friends they just ig - nore me, tell___

— me ne - ver mind, wait - ing all your life for_____ the Slum - ville_ sun - rise.
— me ne - ver mind, wait - ing all your life for_____ the Slum - ville_ sun - rise.

Slum - ville sun - rise,_____ no - bo - dy cares or looks twice._____

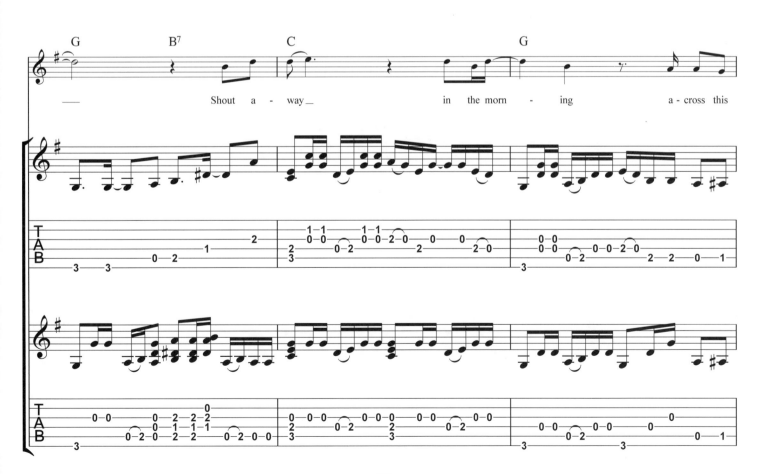

_____ Shout a - way__ in the morn - ing a - cross this

13

place_____ where I____ was born in.____ Ev - 'ry bruise,_ ev - 'ry

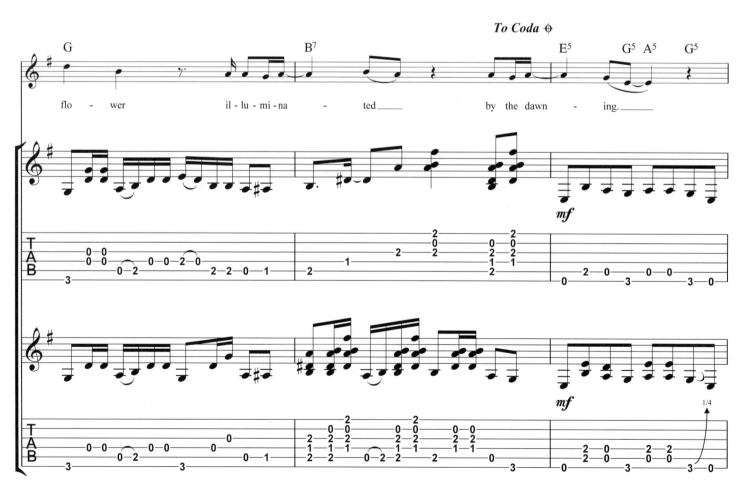

flo - wer il - lu - mi - na - ted____ by the dawn - ing.____

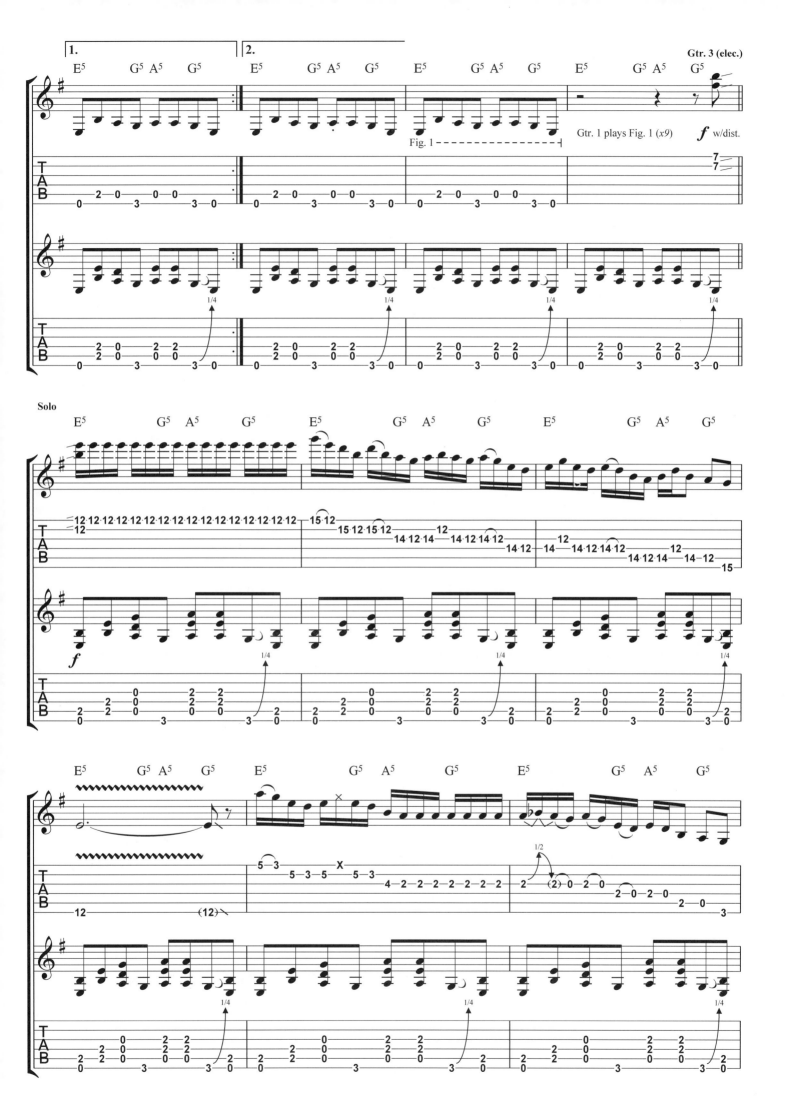

16

flo - wer   il - lu - mi - na - ted_____   by the dawn -

- ing._____

17

WHAT DOESN'T KILL YOU

Words & Music by Jake Bugg & Iain Archer

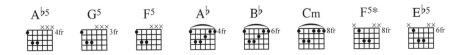

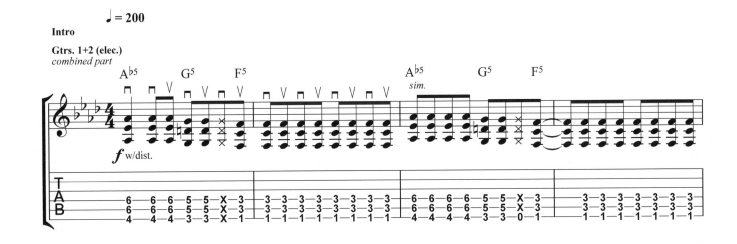

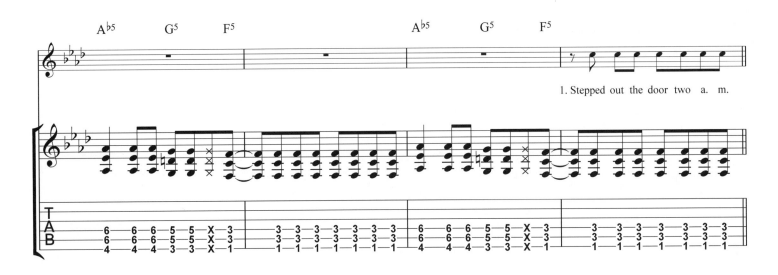

clear lamp light, two guys come up and take him out of sight. ___
dis - ap - peared, my life will be a bunch of sou - ve - nirs. ___

Gtr. 1 *cont. in slashes*

P.M.

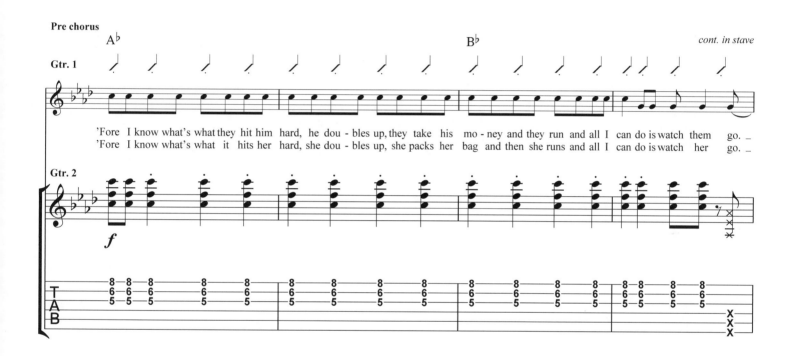

Pre chorus

cont. in stave

Gtr. 1

'Fore I know what's what they hit him hard, he dou - bles up, they take his mo - ney and they run and all I can do is watch them go. ___
'Fore I know what's what it hits her hard, she dou - bles up, she packs her bag and then she runs and all I can do is watch her go. ___

Gtr. 2

f

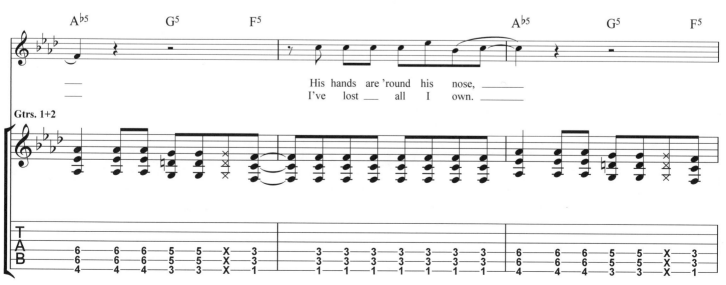

His hands are 'round his nose, ___
I've lost ___ all I own. ___

Gtrs. 1+2

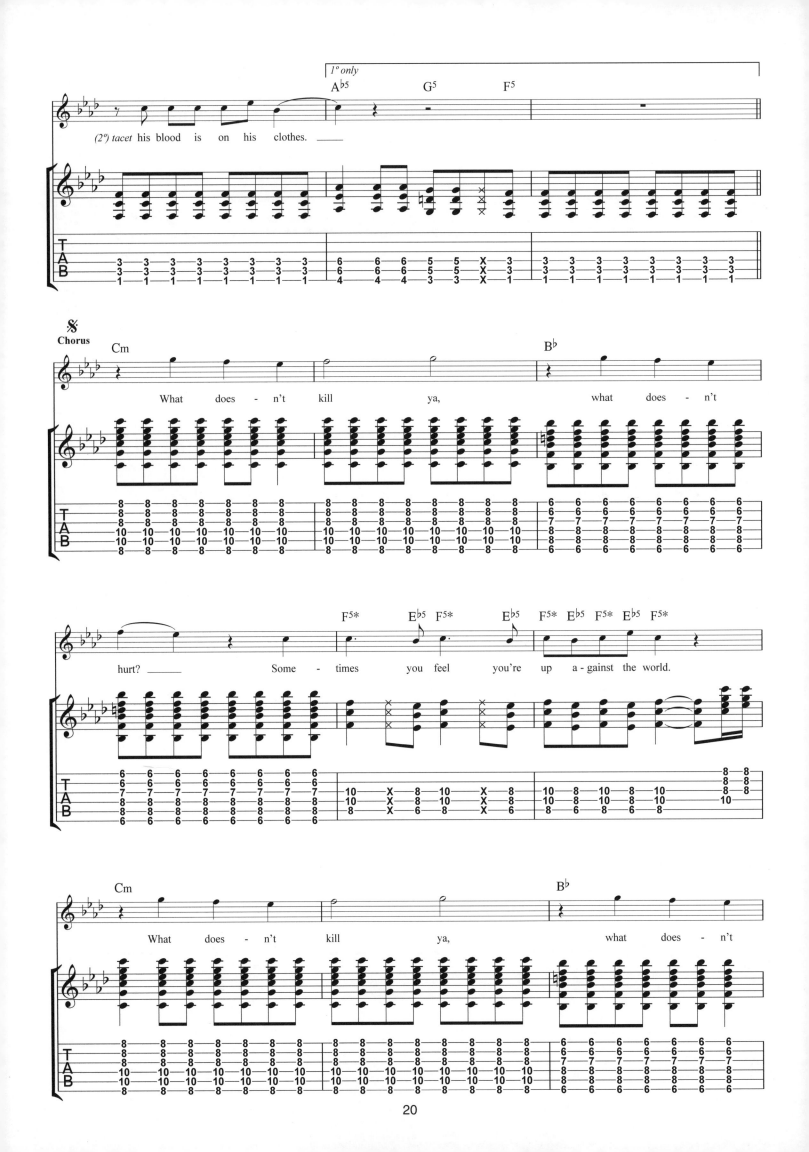

20

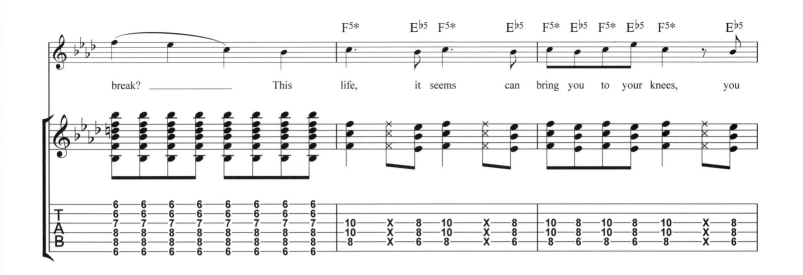

break? _____ This life, it seems can bring you to your knees, you

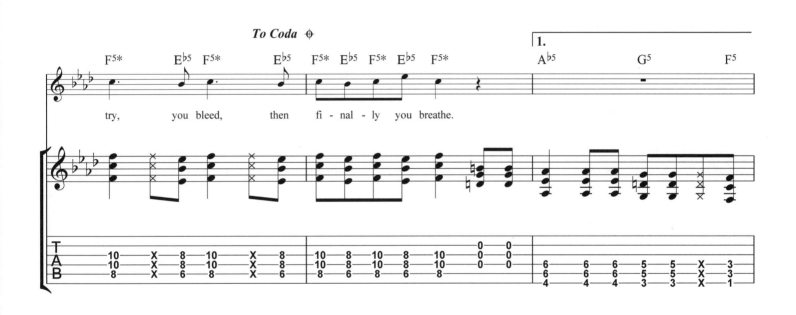

To Coda ⊕

try, you bleed, then fi - nal - ly you breathe.

1.

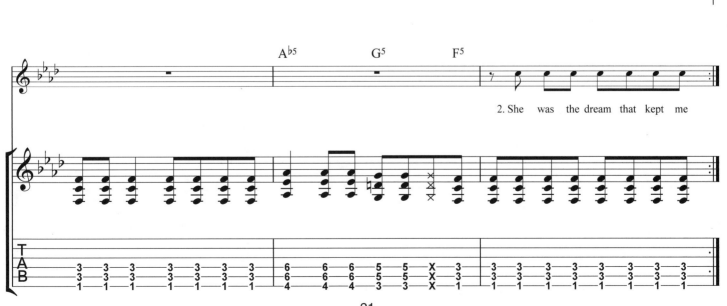

2. She was the dream that kept me

ME AND YOU

Words & Music by Jake Bugg

24

Chorus
Gtr. 1

A (F)

It's all ___ o - ver all of the time ___ and

C#m (Am)

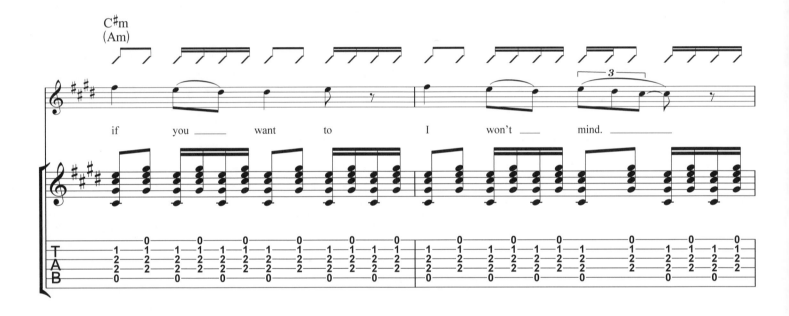

if you ___ want to I won't ___ mind. ___

To Coda ⊕

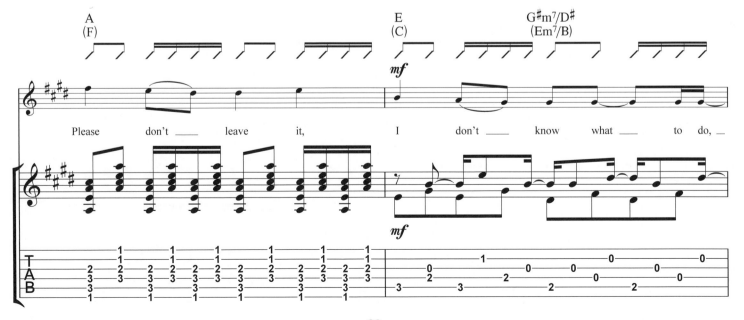

A (F)   E (C)   G#m⁷/D# (Em⁷/B)

Please don't ___ leave it, I don't ___ know what ___ to do, ___

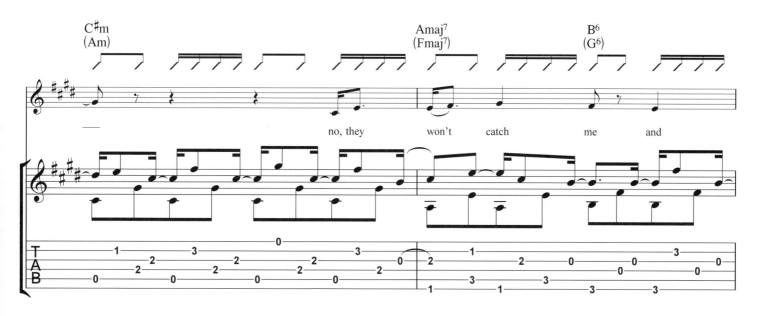

no, they won't catch me and

1.

E
(C)

you.

Gtr. 1 plays Fig. 1

Bridge

2.

E
(C)

mf

All of these peo - ple

C#m
(Am)

Amaj⁷
(Fmaj⁷)

B⁶
(G⁶)

want us to fail, _ I won't let that hap - pen

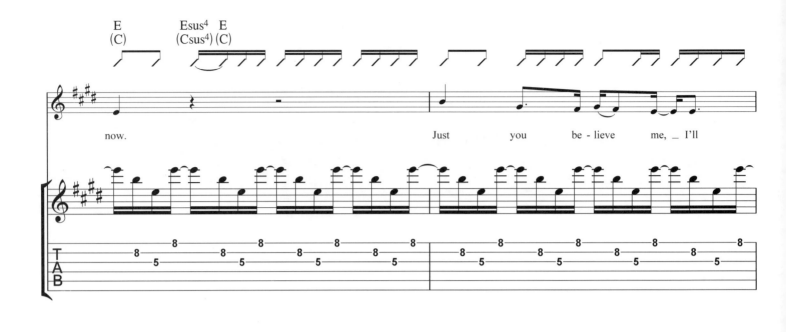

now.   Just   you   be - lieve   me, __ I'll

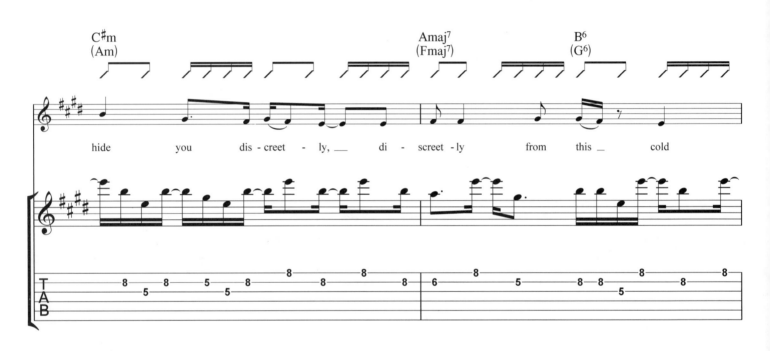

hide   you   dis - creet - ly, ___   di - screet - ly   from   this __   cold

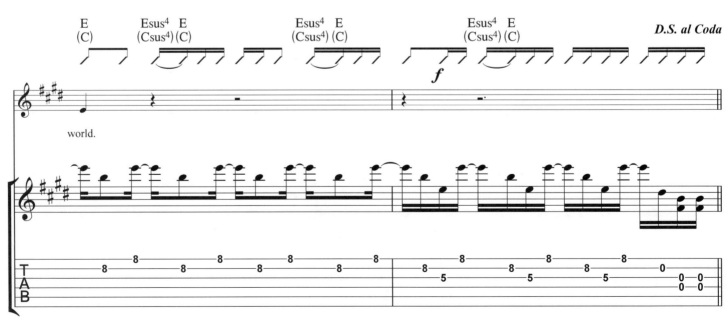

world.

D.S. al Coda

MESSED UP KIDS

Words & Music by Jake Bugg, Iain Archer & Brendan Benson

†Symbols in parentheses represent chord names with respect to capoed guitar.
Symbols above represent actual sounding chords. (TAB 0=6th fret; Gtr. 1)

31

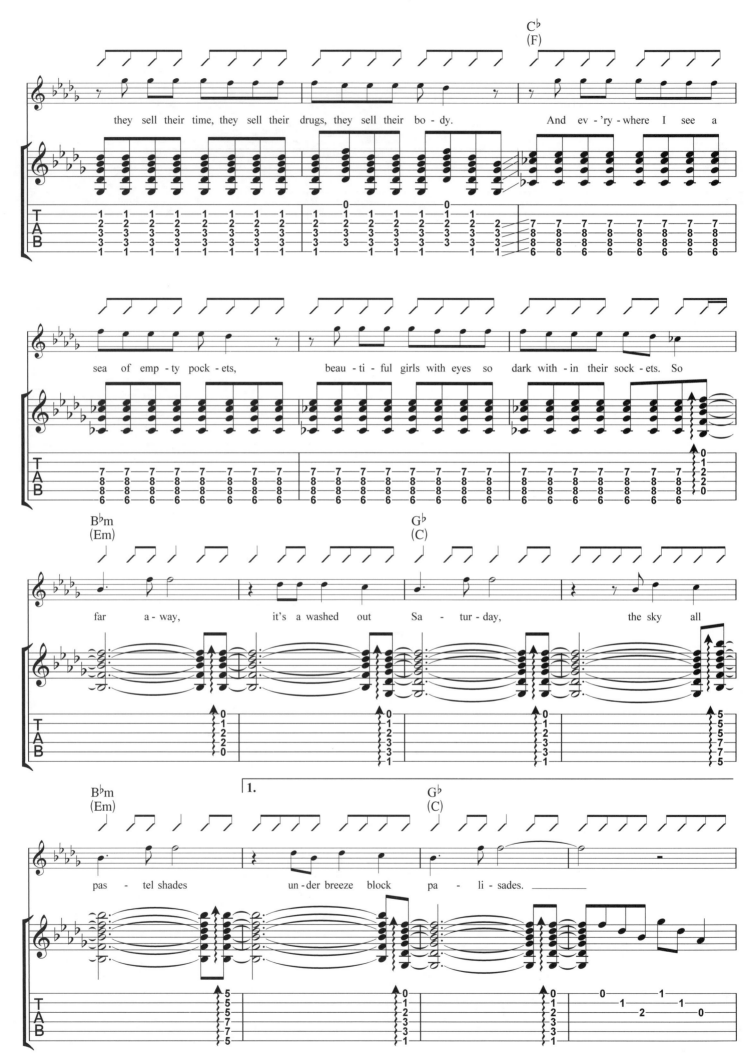

32

33

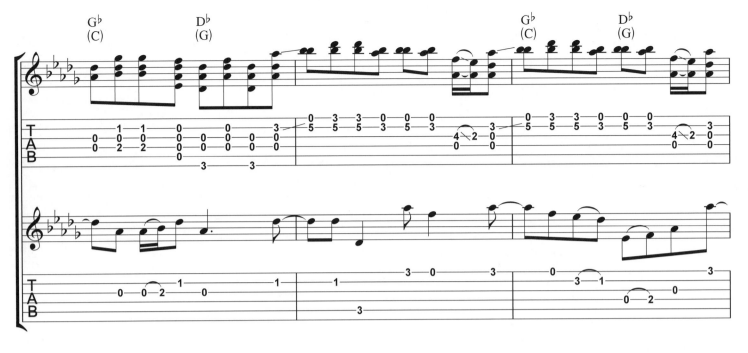

To Coda ✛   *D.S. al Coda*

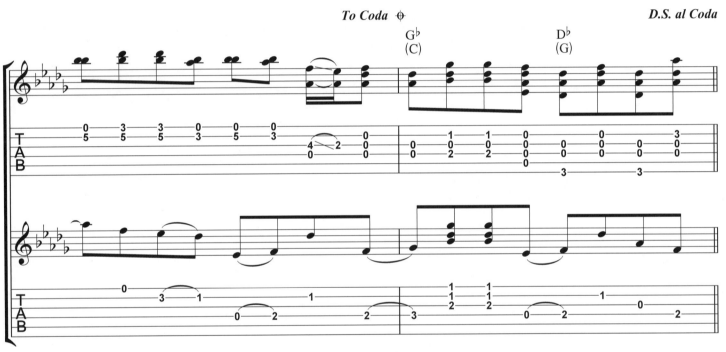

✛ *Coda*

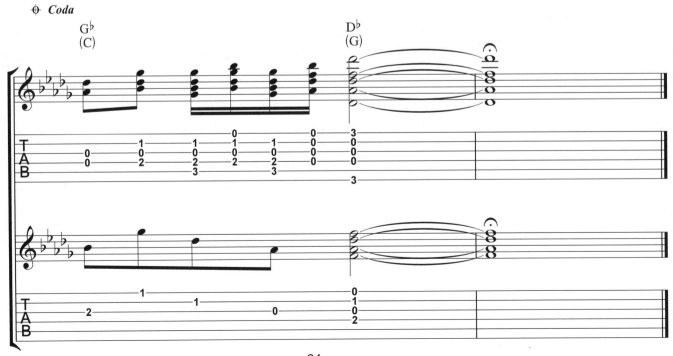

34

A SONG ABOUT LOVE

Words & Music by Jake Bugg & Iain Archer

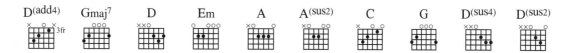

Original recorded key: D♭. To match original recording tune all guitars down a semitone

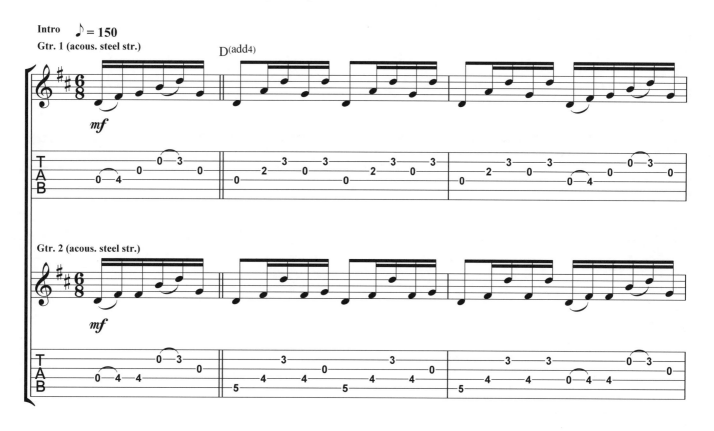

1. You tell me all __ the things

Verse

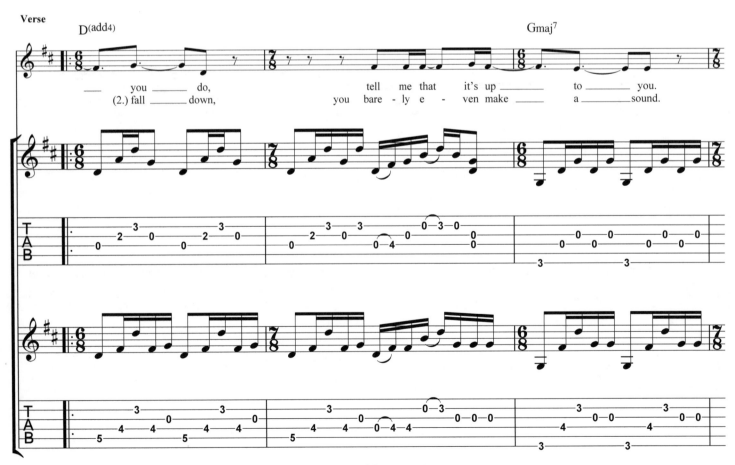

__ you _____ do,   tell   me   that   it's up _____ to _____ you.
(2.) fall _____ down,   you   bare - ly e - ven make _____ a _____ sound.

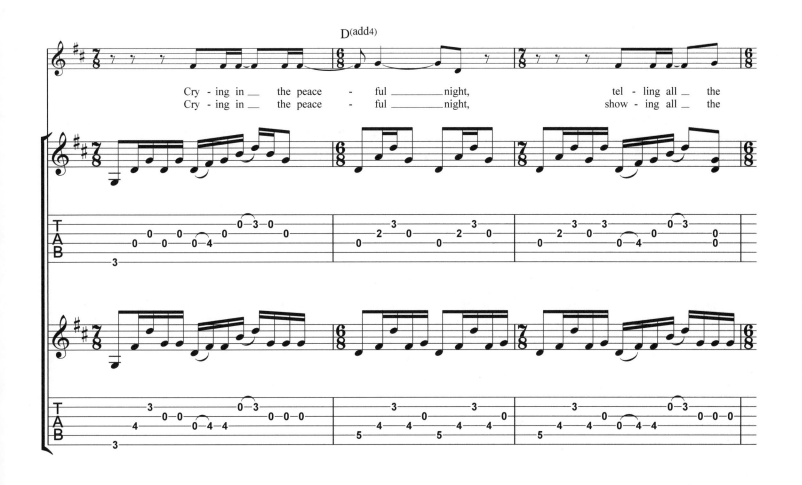

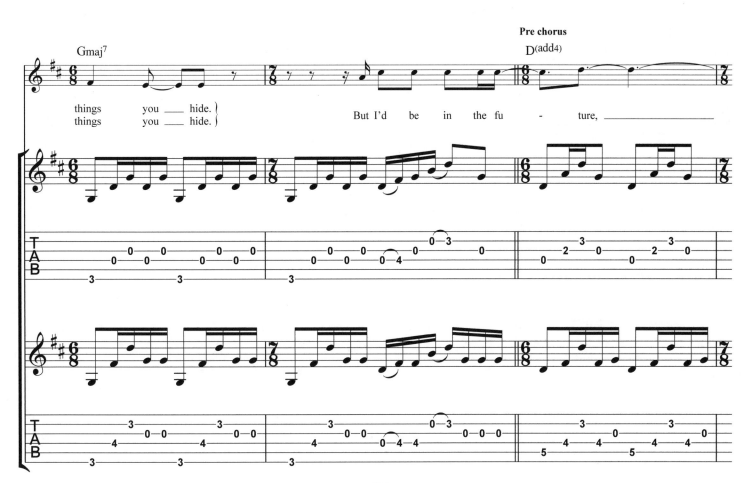

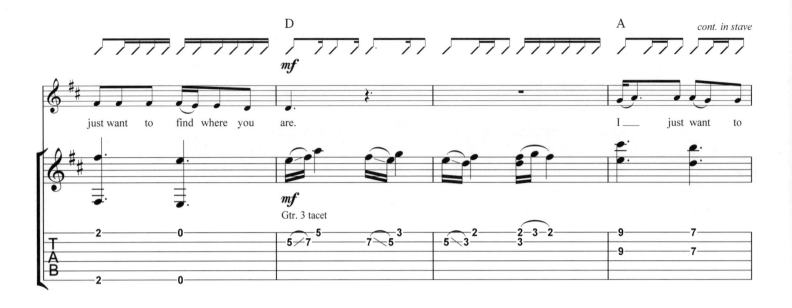

just want to find where you are.

I ___ just want to

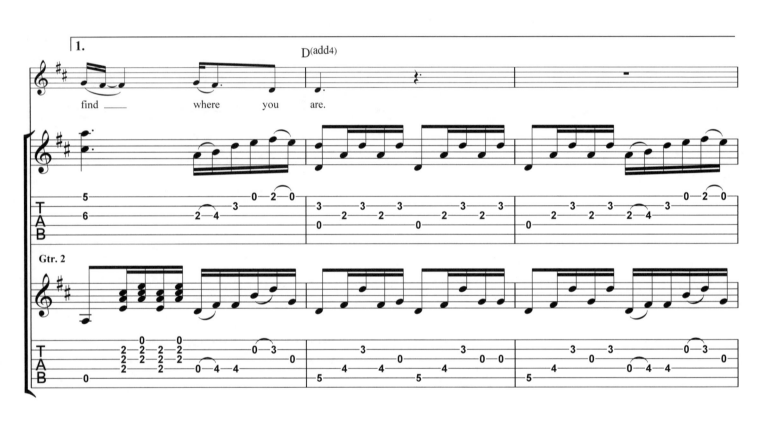

find ___ where you are.

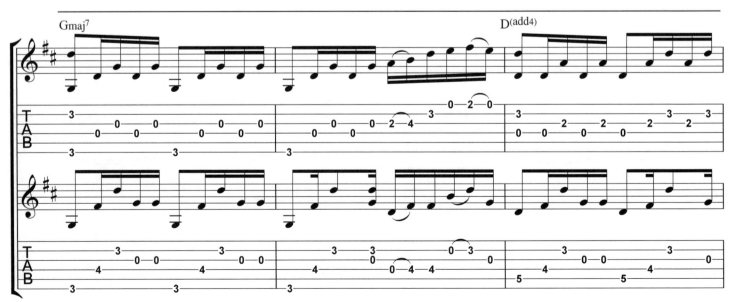

ALL YOUR REASONS

Words & Music by Jake Bugg

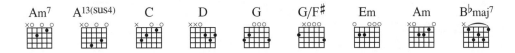

*Original recorded key: Gm. To match original recording tune all guitars down 1 whole tone

Intro

♩ = 148

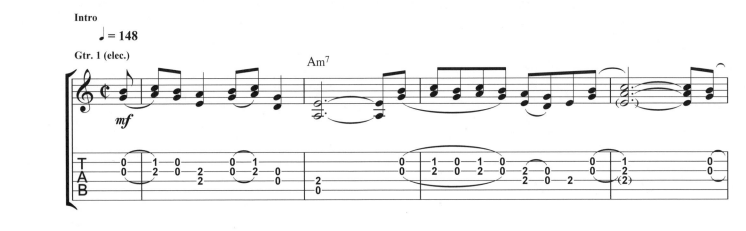

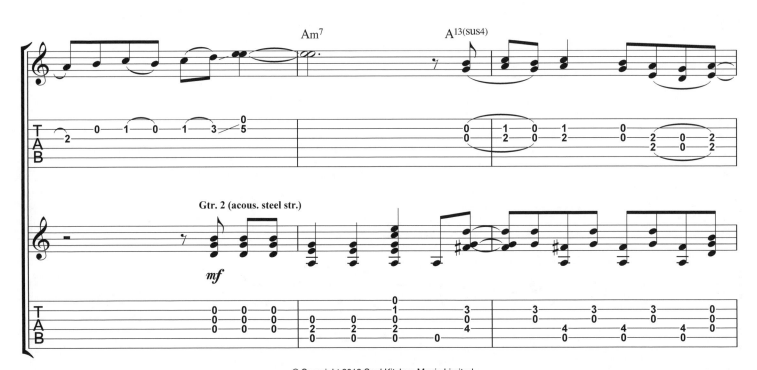

1. Got all of __ your rea - sons __ and all of them's been used, __ I've
2. Did -n't dis - ap - point __ you, did - n't want to make you sad, __
(3.)heard all the __ ex - cu - ses __ and all have been re - fused, __ I've

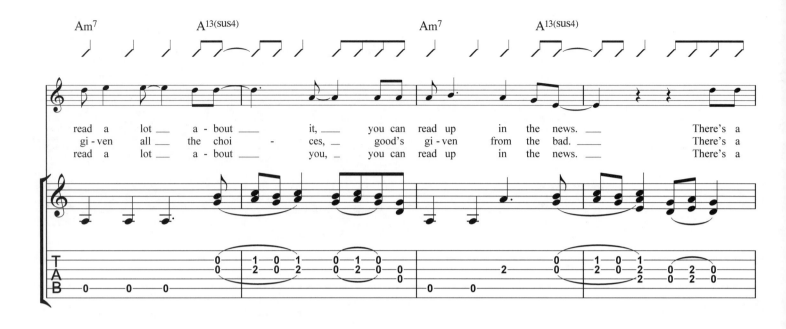

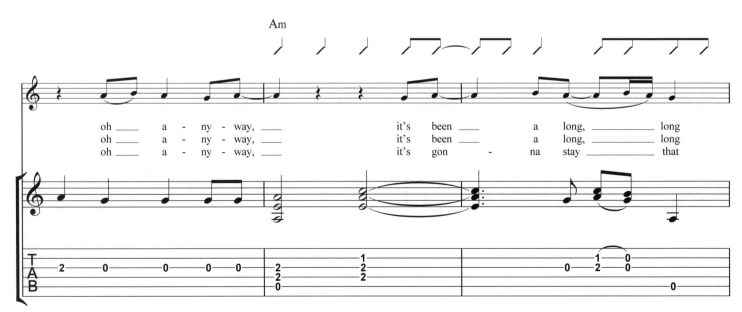

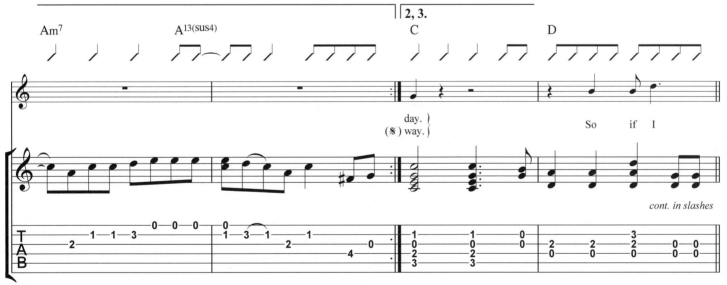

Chorus

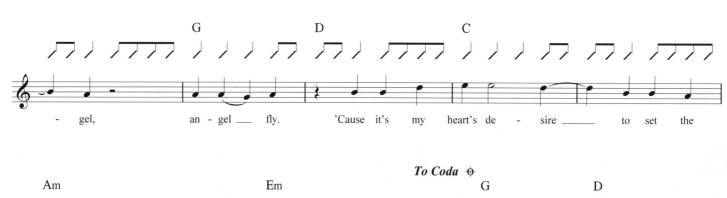

-gel, an - gel ___ fly. 'Cause it's my heart's de - sire ___ to set the

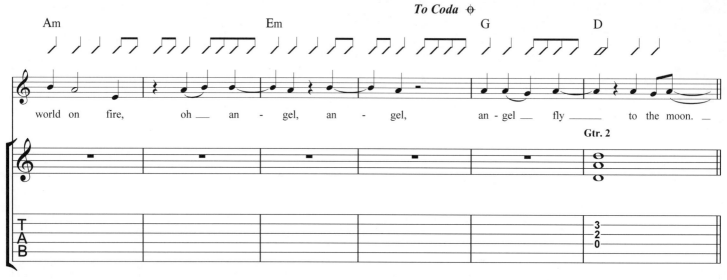

world on fire, oh ___ an - gel, an - gel, an - gel ___ fly ___ to the moon. ___

Bridge

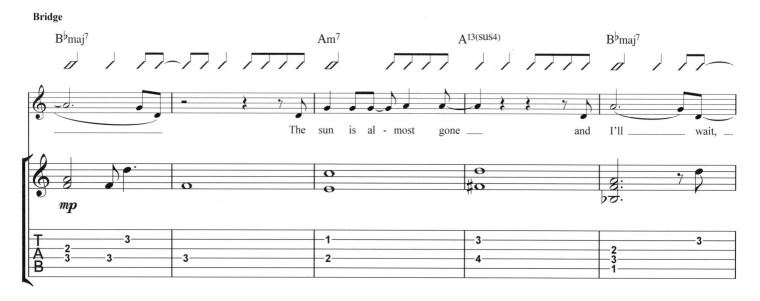

The sun is al - most gone ___ and I'll ___ wait, ___

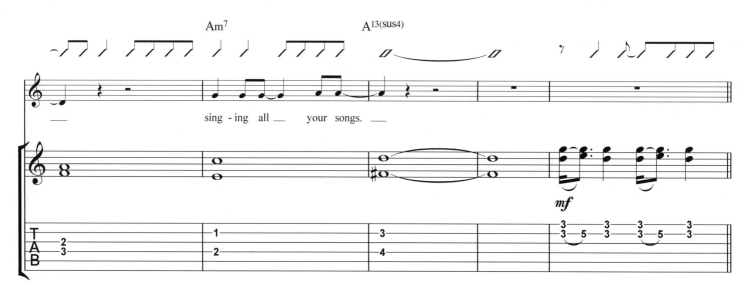

___ sing - ing all ___ your songs. ___

46

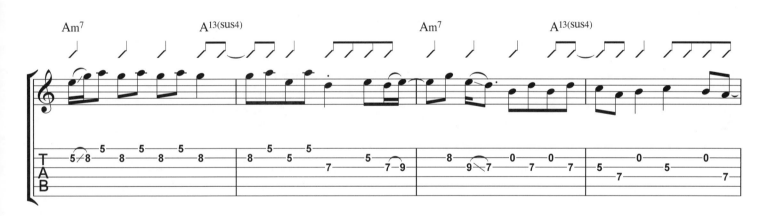

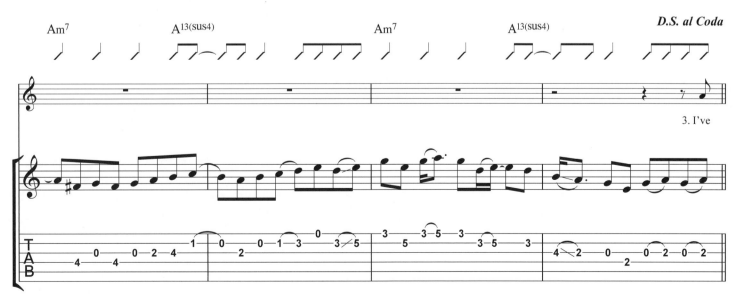

an - gel ___ fly ___ to the moon. _

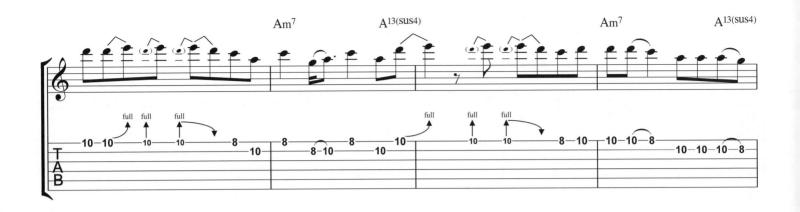
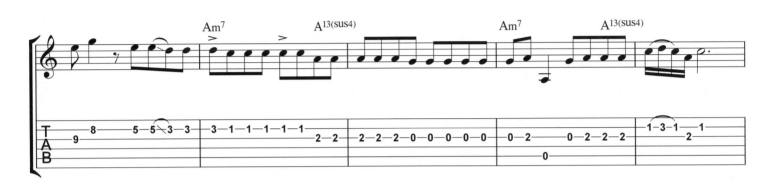

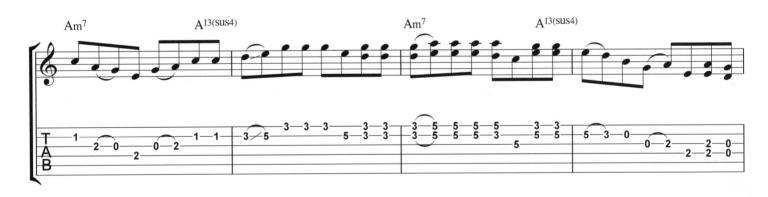

STORM PASSES AWAY

Words & Music by Jake Bugg, Iain Archer & Brendan Benson

it seems ___ you don't need me, where will you
- ance runs deep ___ in my co - lour scheme, where will you

go _____ when the storm pas - ses a - way?⟩
go _____ when the storm wash - es you a - way?⟩

'Cause I'm on ___

Chorus

___ my knees, ___ turn off the dark - ness _ please. ___ Where will you

go?

And they

(2°)'Cause they

keep tell - ing me I'm old - er than I'm s'posed to be, ___ we'll go ___

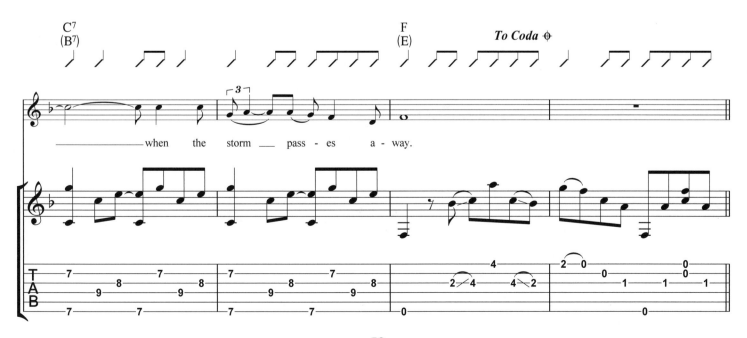

_____ when the storm ___ pass - es a - way.

55

KINGPIN

Words & Music by Jake Bugg, Iain Archer & Brendan Benson

go,   I pay off the po - lice — to stay out of my way. —
- legs,   You'd swear it's from hea - ven, but it all grows na - tu - ral - ly. —
done,   he'll serve it right up to — you on a rus - ty tray. —

—   I got it all sewn up and I'm king - pin for — a day. —
—   I got it all right here and I'm king - pin for — a day. —
—   I don't care a-bout to-mor-row, I'm king - pin for — to - day. —

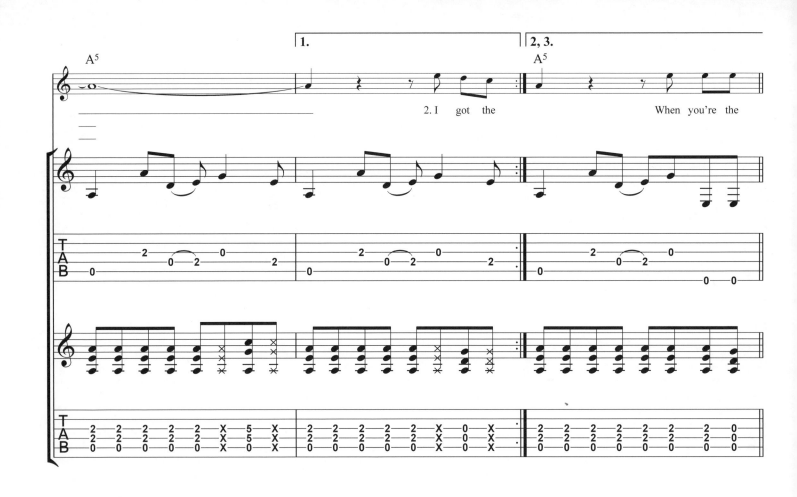

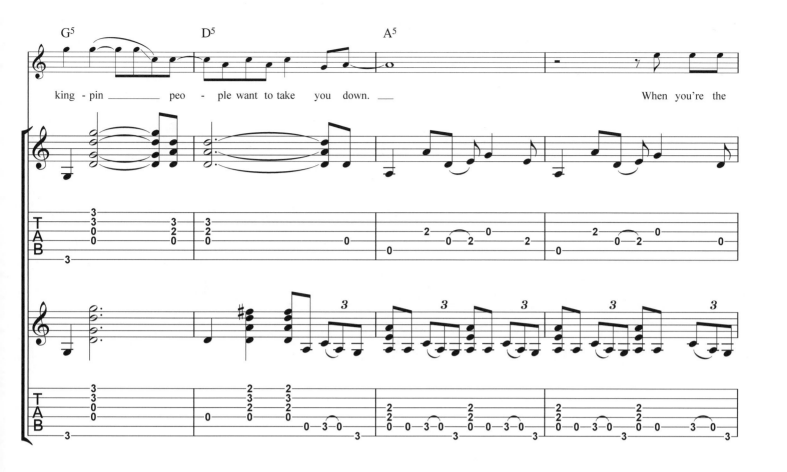

king - pin _____ peo - ple want to take you down. _____ When you're the

king - pin _____ no - bo - dy can show, no - bo - dy can show, no - bo - dy can show you how. _____

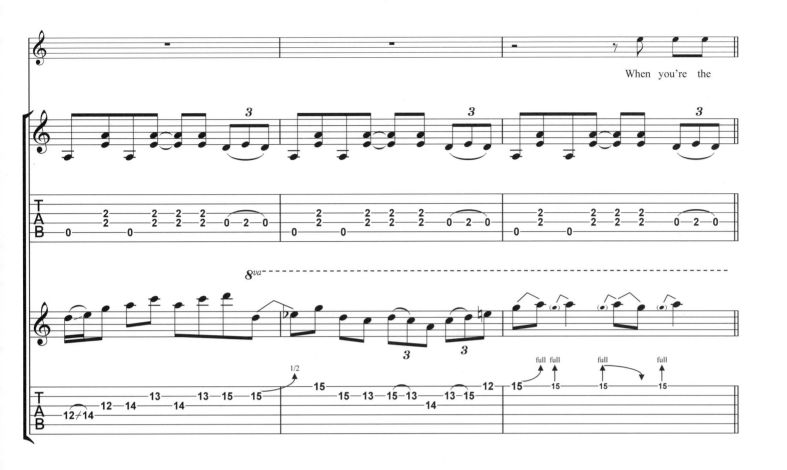

When you're the

Chorus

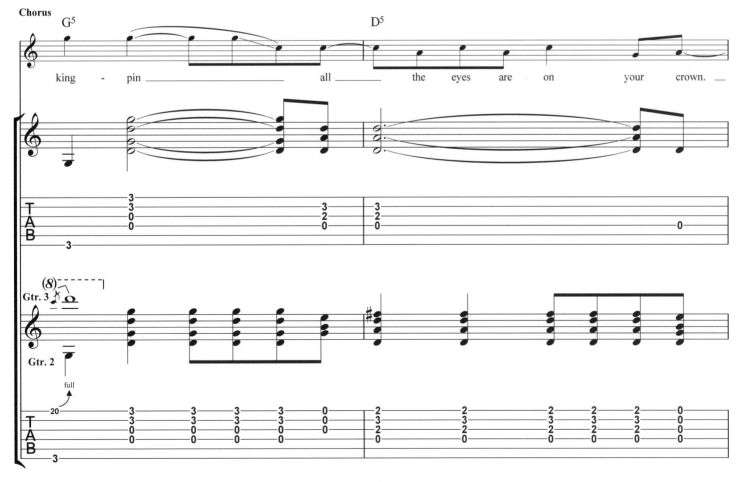

king - pin _____ all _____ the eyes are on your crown. __

When you're the king - pin _____ peo -

- ple want to take   you down. ___   When you're the

KITCHEN TABLE

Words & Music by Jake Bugg

*Chord symbols indicate implied harmony

song by your kit-chen ta - ble, may -be it all ___ seems o - kay. ___ Some -times it's
(2.) rest of the lone - ly peo - ple, ones who live in a cold _dark place. Some -times it's

bet - ter just __ to laugh __ than to run __ a - way. May -be I'll
bet - ter just __ to run __ than to face __ the ___ pain. I've not been

leave you in the co-ming win-ter and all of your dreams soon _ fade a-way. _
see-ing you for _ some time now and still you choose to hold _ my hate. _
(3.) rest of our days to-ge-ther, I may have ne-ver seemed the same. _

_ Some-times it's bet-ter just _ to run _ than to play _ your _ game.
_ But af-ter how I hand-led it _ you're hard-ly to _ blame.
_ Some-times there's no-thing we _ can do _ when we _ all _ change.

When we were lay - ing down __ and you held ____ my hand __ a-mongst the
I feel you read __ my mind and look through __ my soul, __ as ____ our
And now my heart's in two, not a half ____ for you, an - oth - er

o - pal flo - wers, when we sat out - side. __ And now I see it's o - ver now, ____
love grew faint - er and your face grew wet - ter. And I see it's o - ver now, ____
si - tu - a - tion, now the morn - ing's gold - en. And I see it's o - ver now, ____

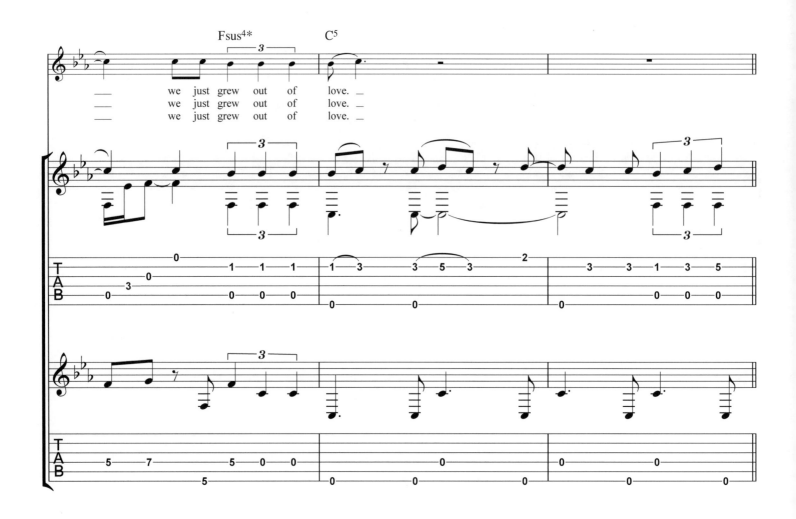

we just grew out of love.
we just grew out of love.
we just grew out of love.

Chorus

Out from the dark-ness your heart-less-ness haunt-ing my fu - ture.

Down on all fours you bark bright at the des-cen-ding moon -

- light.

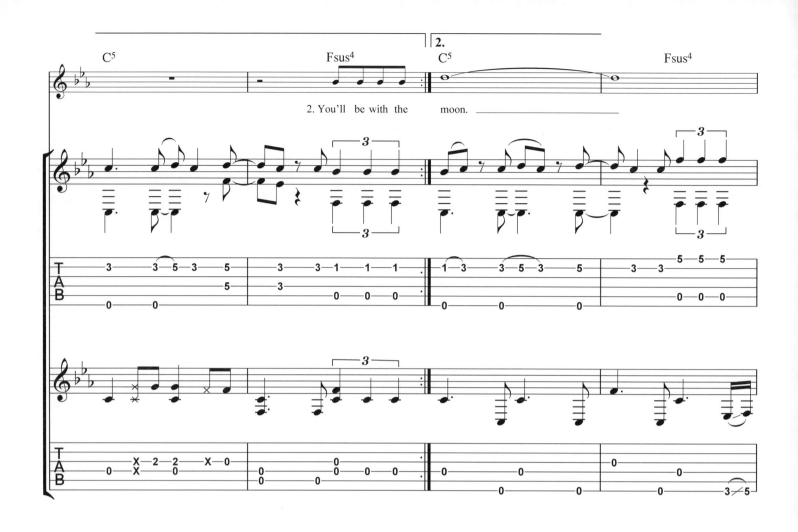

2. You'll be with the moon. _____

Fsus⁴

3. All of the

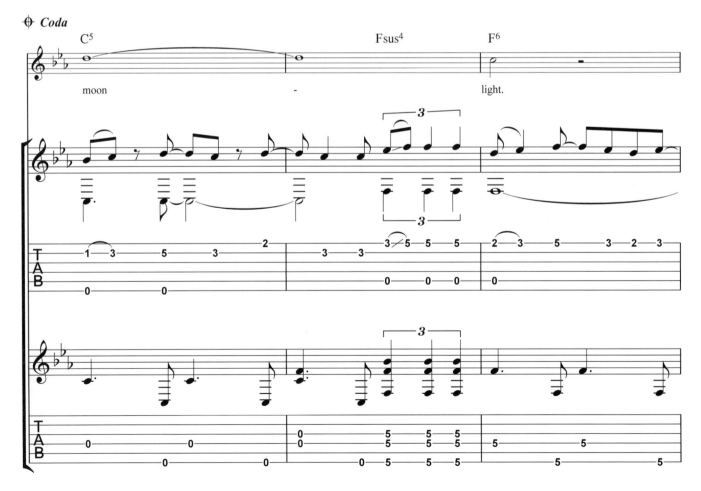

⊕ *Coda*

C⁵ Fsus⁴ F⁶

moon - light.

PINE TREES

Words & Music by Jake Bugg & Iain Archer

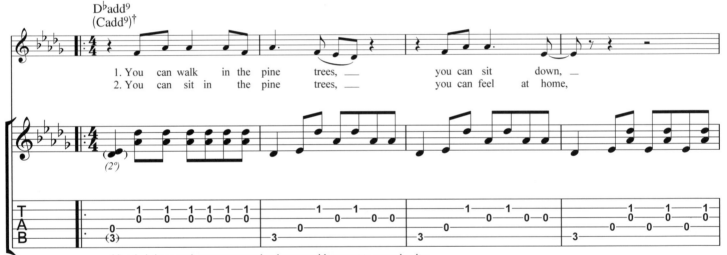

†Symbols in parentheses represent chord names with respect to capoed guitar.
Symbols above represent actual sounding chords. (TAB 0=1st fret)

You can run from all this, ___ you can go the long way,
You can bawl your heart out, ___ make your feel - ings known,

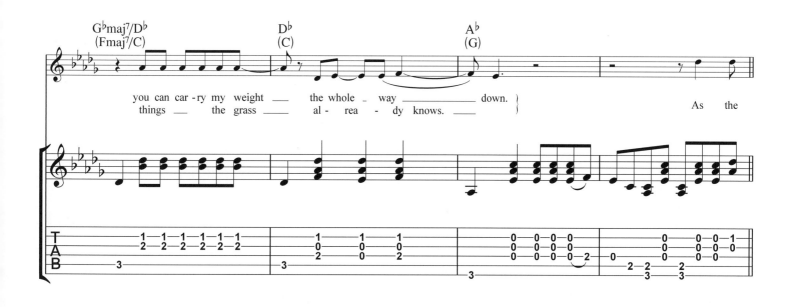

you can car - ry my weight ___ the whole _ way ___ down. }
things ___ the grass ___ al - rea - dy knows. ___

As the

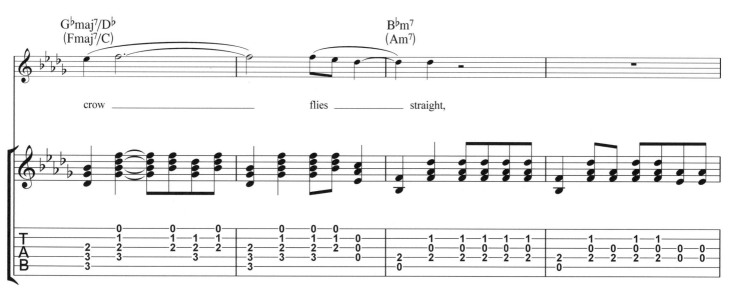

crow _____ flies _____ straight,

SIMPLE PLEASURES

Words & Music by Jake Bugg

†Symbols in parentheses represent chord names with respect to capoed guitar.
Symbols above represent actual sounding chords. (TAB 0=4th fret)

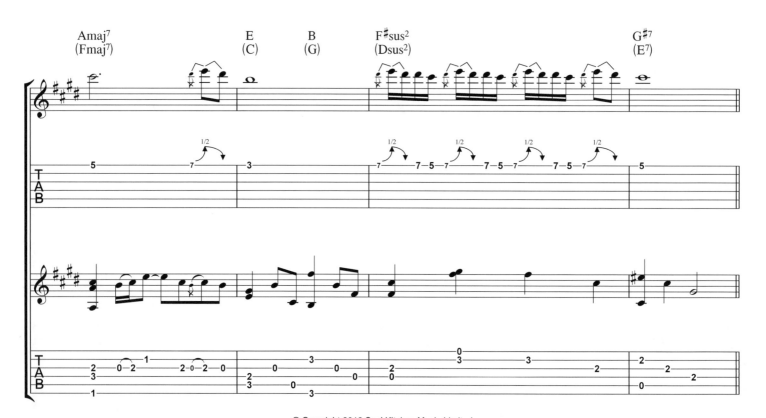

This sud - den fear is strange.

Instrumental

cont. in stave

Gtr. 1

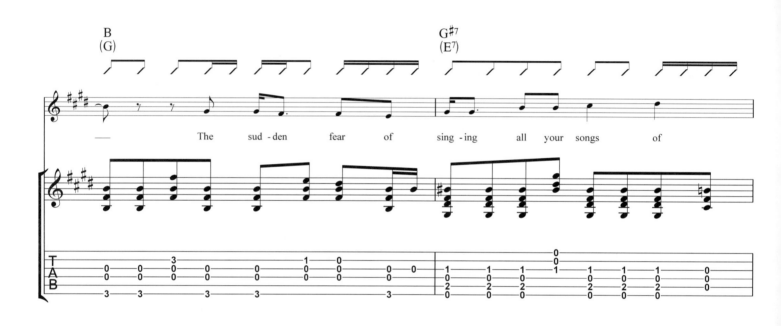

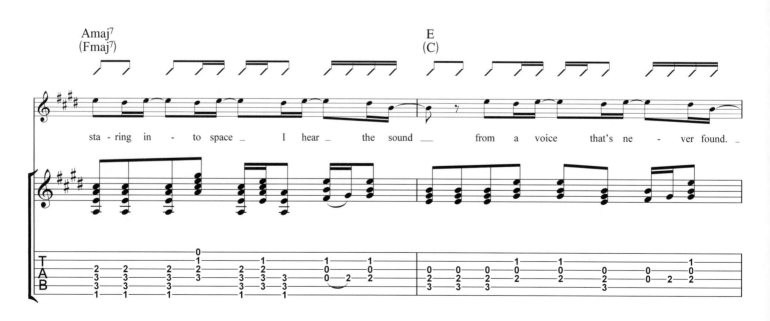

If you like Jake Bugg and bought this book you may also enjoy his first album arranged for guitar tab.

Including the songs:

Lightning Bolt
Two Fingers
Taste It
Seen It All
Simple As This
Country Song
Broken
Trouble Town
Ballad of Mr Jones
Slide
Someone Told Me
Note To Self
Someplace
Fire

Available from all good music retailers.